THE KEY TO YOUR CROWN

Afi kingdom

Table of Contents

FORWARD: BY THE SPIRIT OF MY FATHER

S on, I'm happy to see that you found your passion and your purpose in life! Throughout life I've witnessed you go through adversity. I trust in your spirit, hard work, and determination to give the energy from my spirit to you for the path I've previously laid out. I wish you made it here sooner. The way life is, if it happened any differently we wouldn't have this connection. This conversation was premeditated with acquired experiences that you now have. Where your crown proudly son! I've always seen your potential! The only thing different is that you now see it yourself. You made it! You're now prepared to be great! Live forever…

LESSONS FROM
MY FAILURE

This book is created for you to learn from my failures. Everyone is successful in different avenues, but we all have things that we should work on. In real life, in my opinion people don't reach their full capacity because their ego tells them that they can do it on their own. Some people feel as if they don't need help. This is very foolish, if you look at life in general everyone successful has people that they have met that pushed them to the next level. Think Quincy Jones. He was a very successful composer but the collaboration between him and Michael Jackson made him a legend. Michael Jordan, Phil Jackson. Yes Michael Jordan was considered a great basketball player but until he combined like minds with Phil Jackson the coach he was able to go to the next level. I can go on and on and give you different examples. I'll just give you an assignment. Look at a documentary of your favorite artist, movie star etc.

Once you watch this it will highlight different people in their life, that elevated them spiritually, emotionally or introduce them to a higher playing field. Rihanna was a beautiful woman, teenage Island girl, but she was nothing until she met Jay-Z. He introduced her to the masses, the masses embraced her and she was able to become a superstar. So that's your first assignment. Now the next assignment is not an assignment at all, but it's a mission from me to you. You see I grew up without a father, Yes, I did have father figures. But the difference between now and the internet is you can have online mentors. When I needed someone to help me out I went outside to find that person. This is advice that you should take, as well as other advice I will give you soon. When I say failures I don't necessarily mean things that happened that I'm not proud of. That's just a drastic way for me to make mistakes. But in the context mistakes are minimal. Lot of mistakes you don't care about, you just keep on going. It's the failures that you reflect on.

So that's why I wanted to call this book "lessons from my failures". Just things that I now know in life that I wish someone would have told me. This book can relate to men and women that have daughters or sons and vice versa. This is me talking to my younger self and things that I would wish I would have known. Some things seem obvious, and some things are drastic but everything that I talk about in this book needs to be implemented in your life either immediately, or if you're a young person there things to look at moving forward. I'm giving you clues and secrets to be successful in life. So if this is a woman or man reading this book I'll be your big brother to both of you. I will mentor you through this book and teach you the things that are imperative for your future. Are you ready? Let's begin. Welcome to the Key to your Crown. These are the lessons from my failures....

1

HONOR PARENTS

The first key that I would like to give you to your crown is a simple thing. It may be simple for me but some people may have problems doing this. I feel like it's unfair for people to not honor their parents. And that's just what we're going to do now, we're going to learn how to honor our parents. I know people who come from parents that used drugs, homeless, all of that. I always look at life like it's not about your circumstances it's how you respond to it.

For example someone who comes from a parent with no father can use that as an excuse that he had no guidance and made bad decisions. The next person can use that as the drive to be better than the person that they came from. The key is you came from this person. No matter how bad you want to look at it, without your parents there is no you. Now I'm not saying that you need to go over and throw your mother and father a parade, which isn't a bad idea every now and then. I'm just saying show them respect while they're alive. I've known plenty of people who have lost their parents on bad terms. Mothers and Fathers. After this effect they live the rest of my life with a lot of regret. Don't let this happen to you. Respect your parents while they're here. If you are an adult reading this book you understand that there are times where you may have not done the right thing. And when you look back you wish you could have changed things. For some people who have dysfunctional relationships, your parents may actually feel the same way. Understand that everyone is not a communicator. It's my job as a teacher, author and consultant to listen and understand people. Keyword that it's my job. You would be surprised to see how many grown ass adults don't know how to articulate their feelings. They only know how to communicate anger, frustration and emotion. Please ladies and gentlemen honor your parents while they're here. I understand circumstances hearing people say that their parents were bad and they hate them. Unless it's a case where you were touched inappropriately or super disrespected I understand it may be difficult but should at least respect your parents. Even then if you have a situation like this, you can love something and not deal with it. For the people who don't have a mother and father in their life I understand that I grew up with only a mother. Sure there are people in your life that we're your mentors to help guide you at one point in your life that you respect. Some people were raised by their grandmothers or foster parents Etc. Whoever these people were, who gave you food, knowledge and a place to live honor these people. When things evolve and life changes, living with regret is one of the worst things that you can do. It should put a smile on your face knowing that you were the one to make someone else's day other than your own sometimes. Honor your parents guys. If you have a sticky situation that you feel I may not be able to relate to at least respect them for creating you. You don't know their true story and what made them who they are. You only are aware of what was shared. Ask yourself "do you share everything"?

Probably not! Lastly when you get to honor your parents make it also a point to ask them how they feel sometimes. A lot of times, even myself I get wrapped up in my own life and forget to check in on the people who love me. Just make it a point to check in with the people you love and respect, and can even figure out ways to spend time and create new experiences together.

My mother has never been to Miami before. So by the time she reads this book I probably will have the reservations already taken care of. I can pay for my mother to go to Miami for her by herself obviously. But I feel like she would get more out of the deal if she had this experience along with me. The smile on her face is enough to keep me going, planning something for us both to look forward to. You only live one life, don't live the rest of it being petty, or in denial of anything. We live one life, so I understand you have to pick your battles. Ask yourself, is it worth it? Usually the answer is no. It will be the moments that you create that will smile and motivate you in the darkest times of your life. Respect honor your parents and family, start creating these new moments.

2

FIND SOMETHING TO LIVE FOR

One of the most important keys I feel like is having something to live for. I have a lot to live for. I want success, I want to provide for my family and I want to live in abundance. People assume that you work very hard just to have money, flex, stunt on Instagram to look famous. I'm literally chasing my freedom and that's all I care about. Money really isn't the issue I just want to be able to do whatever I want whenever I want. I always talk to people who are rich and I think that is funny how they think. I feel like once you get to a certain level we can all do the same stuff. If I have 1 million, and you have 1.2 million technically yes you have more money than me. But we can live the same lifestyle, buy the same cars, and live in the same house. So it's not a particular number that I'm chasing. I'm just chasing the feeling when I can work for myself only, not just doing great work so other people can tell me "great job", but doing the work for myself to progress in my own life. That's what I want to do. So what is it that you want to live for?

In order to be successful you have to get in detail. I'm going to give you opportunities to write these things down. Not only are you going to write these things down but you're going to write them down in this very book. I'm going to hold you accountable for these things. So I want you to look at this as your diary from now on. You're not writing for an assignment. Not for a grade. You're writing to access yourself and your goals. Everything that you want out of life. I want you to dig a Little Deeper. A million dollars, a big house and a Mercedes Benz is 50% of people's answers. Ask yourself exactly what you want. Do you want a townhouse, a duplex, a wooden house?. Do you want a Bentley or a Bentley truck with purple Lamborghini doors and Red

Spinners. I don't think that you would want that car, but what I'm asking you to do is write in detail everything you want out of life and reflect on it. Figure out an action plan of how you can get these things. And if you're a young person let this be your journal to reflect on throughout your life and your adolescent years until adulthood. A lot of people aren't successful! Even myself, because you don't have a plan of how I would get there I just wanted it. Most of my life I knew I wanted to be successful but I didn't have the steps to get there. All that I know is I wanted to be a principal, write a book and direct a movie. Now I'm in a position where I can do two of those things just with my career as a podcaster. I could still be a principal as well ,but I feel after writing books and directing movies, teaching kids, and my needy dogs, having children of my own is the last thing I want to spend my energy on because it requires so much. That's because I'm spending energy on other people, things that are our energy building for myself, my future, maybe children, grandchildren. What my mind says now is that I can either put my time in and evolve someone's company or brand or I can spend the same energy doing it myself. The difference between working for yourself is when you fail you get back up. When you fail at a job you get fired. Entrepreneurship obviously isn't for everyone. But I feel like in life you need to try things before you say it isn't for you. Get a taste of the long hours because you will work long more than a 9 to 5. You can start by selling clothes. Things that you don't wear in your closet , have a garage sale. That will give you a sense of having something of value and people paying you for it. Off the clock. These are just a few keys. I'm not telling you how to live your life just giving you ideas as well as telling you a little bit of how I would like to live mine. Find something to live for….

3

WORK OUT

W orking out is another simple one. Now you may think of course "I know how to work out what you think I am an idiot". No I don't think you're an idiot, but what I will tell you is that if you are in the habit of working out as a lifestyle, then you don't have to get in shape. Even me right now. I want to lose about 20 lbs and gain maybe 15 pounds of muscle mass. The point is if I was trying to work out at an early age and made it become my routine I would already be in shape. I wouldn't have to backtrack the way that I am doing now. I use this for an example….

As people know if you're familiar with my books and content I usually read about a book a week. At this point in my life I've been a little bit busy or being a creator, so I read about two maybe three a month instead of four. So now I will usually read between two books at a minimum and 3 out of Max. The point is, reading has been a part of my routine since I was an early child. My mother read to me when I was very young and made me read to her as well.

Iceberg Slim was the first book that I read when I was 9 years old. That book was very thick with no pictures. But I was already having a habit of reading daily, which my mother implemented in me. It wasn't a big deal to read that book because it was already a part of my routine. It was a new experience that I felt that I wanted to learn. The fact that it was a small book that was so thick it intrigued me, and I knew I was reading something that a nine-year-old shouldn't be able to read. This was my Big Brother's book. Do you ever wonder when you see "gym rats" and you think damn how did they spend all their time in the gym that's all they do. All they do is eat, sleep, and work out. That's because it's their routine. If you have a routine early of looking good and feeling good it will do multiple things for you.

It's the first thing you can do that will make you feel good. If you work out it's always a rush feeling once you finish. Having that feeling of completion every single day means a lot. Even in the dating world there are a lot of people who are not attractive men and women, that get away with a lot and even can get high-value mates just for having a nice body. So stop complaining about how your face looks bad and you weren't blessed the way other people on TV or movie stars are. If you work on that body you'll be alright. This goes for males and females. Working out will also create a healthy lifestyle for you and if you really work out you may even find healthy companions who live similar lifestyles than you. Being around people that are positive and have healthy active lifestyles will produce high frequency energy and you will accomplish many goals this way.

Don't get in shape, stay in shape and make it your routine. I myself have lost up to 85 lbs. I can't tell you the feeling that I had looking at those before and after pictures. It's okay to make mistakes and back track. That happens in life. But I'm telling you now, if you're young work out, start at an early age. If you make working out a part of your life. I can almost guarantee you not that you won't be perfect, but if you mark on the calendar on the 1st and you consistently workout for 6 months to June 1st you will feel and look better. I will put my life on this. Workout!!!

4

STUDY READ LANGUAGE

gain as you see ,these things are simple. However I can almost guarantee you that they're not a part of your routine. Keyword routine. You are studying for a test, or are you reading a book because someone gave you a book and told you it was interesting. That is not your routine. Routine is daily and weekly. You need to be studying things on a daily basis. Personally, I spend a lot of time studying content. The kind of content that I watch, the way they make content, what's successful and what is not. When I watch podcasts I watch how the people ask questions, how the person responds to it, even how people sit. When I study these things I go back and readjust my own content as I do podcasts myself. I study other people. I don't just go off of what I think feels good I look and see what works and what doesn't.

Where I educate it is in the Hispanic environment. Now some children are small and I'm always fascinated that a kids 6 years old or even younger five or four can speak multi languages. Yet I'm grown and I can only speak one. I understand that when you're younger you can take up things, but if I can do it all again or if I had my own child I will make them study another language. It's imperative. Learn another language! When I finish all 13 of my books that will be the first thing that I do. But it's not a part of my immediate plan because I have to get these 13 books done first. But I will learn another language for sure. Just the way people treat you and look at you. Think about when you see someone and they speak another language how cool it is. Especially a child, how cool it makes them look when they are speaking a language of a decent that is not their own. Not only that it just gives you options in life. Reading is not just fundamental like the saying is, but it also can save your life. Get in the habit of reading just to live through other people's experiences.

You will notice patterns in life that a lot of people end up in similar circumstances and situations. Look at how they handled it, and think about how you can handle it or if the situation may be coming up think of how you can handle it better than they did. That my friend will get you to our next level of success. Not only should you be reading, but you should be picking up different kinds of books. If you like books that are funny don't only read books that are funny. A quick story I used to think golfing was only for white people. I'm not being racist I'm just being honest. A co-worker of mine exposed me to that and now it's something that I love. Be open to other people's ideas in life and even if you don't agree, look and try to understand where they're coming from. I will suggest picking one book of every single genre. Or let's start you off slowly from now on, no matter how old you are and how busy you are I want you to read at least one book a month. I will explain to you how to do this in the later chapter. Some people read a book and once they finish that book they won't read another one for another five six months. Maybe when their favorite celebrity or athlete puts out their bio they'll pick that one up. Wrong. Read a recipe book in January. Read a novel in February. Try a love story for March. In November try finding a book of the history of Thanksgiving. These small gems will make you a deeper intellectual and you will be able to meet and connect with more people of every race and background. Read books. Study. And lastly work on another language. These will take you to the next stratosphere!

5

PRACTICE CONVERSATION

P racticing conversation can exponentially change your life. This is the lesson that I'm learning right now. As I'm learning to be an entrepreneur I observed that conversation is key. Life is all about connections and meeting the right people. If you haven't mastered this then you're almost living life, flipping a coin, hoping that you will be discovered doing something great. Being a coach for the past three years I come across a lot of successful guys that are socially awkward. I never really understood that this was a problem. I would hear about women complaining about guys that were socially awkward, had no game, and never having things to say. Since my mouthpiece is strong, I couldn't really relate to it. It took for me to start coaching to see the other side.

For whatever reason some people really have problems talking to people. If you want to throw the dating in there, that's a whole extra ball game. I have two or three books actually dedicated to dating so I would really rather reference those books for you to get instead of giving that wisdom to you here. I once read in a book, and I can't tell you what book it was, but basically they said that you were 3 people away from the person that would help you become the best version of yourself. It's kind of like Usher the R&B singer. When he started off he was under Puff Daddy's lead. That's person number one. The second person would be JD, which he would take him under his wing and turn him into a superstar. That's person number two. Person number 3 is the audience that you were introduced to from these chain of events. Networking is key, some people get lucky. They're talented in singing or skills which everyone, actually the majority of people in life are not going to do. But if you have a mouthpiece and you're not scared to use it, you don't need talent, you just need to know what to say and who you say it to.

But how can you do these things that I mention if you haven't practiced the skill of conversation? I recommend you talking to multiple people a day. I will break it down to a science on the next piece. From this day forward you should not go without greeting people when in contact. Now if you really want to get good you can go out of your way to talk to people but I don't have that expectation from you. When you lock eyes though however learn to speak. Not only do you need to learn to speak but learn to reply to what they say. Then you shall have a conversation. When you have enough conversations you will learn how to control them too. See the capabilities of where they can go from recognizing patterns as I always say. Don't be scared to talk because a closed mouth doesn't get fed. Remember that you can be the best at whatever it is that you're doing, but if no one knows who you are then where would that leave you? Once you get into the habit, your energy will make people start conversations with you. Remember the more Focus that you have like I said prior, the more interesting things you do, the more people will be interested in you.

Once you understand that you, you will be inspired to master your conversations as well as create more opportunities to speak. Shit why you think I started a podcast. Practice what you preach and keep preaching it. Learn, practice, and master conversation.

6

EMBRACE PEOPLE BETTER
THAN YOU

I will explain to you why embracing people better than you is imperative. I feel a lot of times in the competitive nature of men and women we spend most of our time competing. As they say it's always easier to build a house with more hands. People often find themselves insecure, unable to show their weaknesses. They often only want to show their strengths. Now logically this seems like a good thing, but what happens is you don't improve on your weaknesses because you are only proud of what you're good at. Instead of competing with people, like they are in race with you, try to embrace people that are better than you.

If you listen to any significant author, personal development coach, or things of that nature they will all tell you or speak about a mentor that they had in life. That's because they were smart enough to not hate, be jealous and actually embrace people that were better than themselves. When I say embrace people that are better than you, I don't mean better as a whole. Just better at something that you may lack. Whatever it is that you're trying to get better at there is someone better than you and if you have good energy and also provide value they will help you in what they lack. It's providing value for value. I run a consulting firm. So if I need a website instead of stressing myself out I can reach out to someone who may need help with their mindset but they have a skill that I can't do myself. That's what value for value is. I'm humble enough to know that someone is better than me at a particular thing and I embraced the fact that they can help me do it. They can either help me or show me. But a lot of times it's much easier for someone that teaches you hands-on then it is to try to frustrate and learn yourself.

Mastermind groups are the best. I'm in a few! With these groups there are people of all trades, all shapes and sizes, who are masters in particular things. It could be trading, Bitcoin, or even health. Everyone is a master in their trade and being a Mastermind Group, you have access to all these excellent Beautiful Minds. I'm intelligent to know that if I want to be successful in life I have to embrace people better than me. When I acquire skills that they show me through their actions, teachings or just watching their experiences. I could also pay it forward to others.

I'm the type of person once I master something I can't wait to teach it. This is because you're not a master at anything until you can teach it to someone else. It's just like creating content on YouTube. You can live this lifestyle and do all the things that you think will get viewers and attention. Entertaining the crowd, keeping them coming back and consistently coming up with engaging topics and engaging content is more difficult than people often imagine. On top of that, this field is oversaturated and has a lot of competition. There is much more competition I say, five six years ago when I first started watching this kind of content.

Always remember to embrace people better than you. You can win the race for yourself but don't let your ego get in the way of just asking for help. Not everyone is against you. Not everyone wants to see you lose. Trust there are plenty of people who want to see you win. But in order to have that experience you must embrace these people. You must embrace people better than you. That is if you would like to become better. If you are on your purpose, have a good spirit, and positive energy you may search but also these people will come to you. Keep an open mind and be willing to learn from everyone. Embrace you. Embrace education. Embrace others. Most importantly, Embrace your crown

7

TAKE CARE OF YOU

T aking care of you can be number one in a lot of people's minds. A lot of people don't put themselves first. When I say take care of yourself I mean everything. But what I want to focus on is just things that you can do yourself. The bare necessities. You'd be surprised how many grown-ups don't even know how to cook for themselves. I'll use myself for example. My mother always cooks for me to the extent where even though I know how to cook, I was used to someone doing it for me and it enabled me. Do things like this: cook for yourself, clean for yourself. It will make you a better person and also when you're in a relationship you won't have to rely on these skills from the other person you're in a relationship with.

Learn how to wash your own clothes. It's obvious as it seems, as I've been coaching for years there's people who lack these things. Maybe it's because it's their significant other that takes care of these chores. They may have a mother or father who take care of all these needs. Simple things, pay your own bills. I've known grown ass men who were 30 years old and the only bill they have is their damn phone bill. I told him if I was 30 and all I had was a phone bill I wouldn't feel like a man. It boils down to this. If you don't have bills you don't have responsibilities. So how can you be responsible without responsibilities?

Completing small tasks for yourself gives you structure and makes you complete small tasks as a habit. When kids are frustrated when their parents tell him to clean that room that's because they're not usually required to do it. They don't want to do it because they're not used to it. Little things like this will make you a better person moving forward. Make sure that you teach them to your kids also if you choose to have them. So many people are dependent on others for things that they could have done their own self. So as of today, untrain yourself to be reliant on others to do simple tasks that you can do for yourself. Before you ask them for your help just pause for a second and think can I do it myself?

If you're the type of person who's always hitting people up for rides ask yourself is this helping? It doesn't matter if you're paying for gas, it's something that you can do yourself. It's just a form of independence. Why would you want to be sitting around waiting for someone else to do something for you at their convenience when you should have your own options. Catching public transportation will help you get more familiar with your area and places that you wouldn't normally go. You could even find alternative routes and cool things to do by passing up lots of places.

Surprisingly, I also know grown people who do not drive. This is ridiculous, if you are healthy and you have nothing wrong with you get up and learn how to drive. I'll give a pass for not having a car if you live in San Francisco or New York but you still should know how to drive. Emergencies can occur. If you're an adult you're not living life. Driving is one of the most independent experiences that you can have that you are not experiencing because you're lazy. Sometimes it's good to take a long drive and reflect on your life and your plan, and it's not going to be fun waiting for your friend to pick you up in order to have this simple experience. People, just take care of yourself and practice being independent. When you think you want to do something, try to do it yourself first. Most of the time you will find that you didn't need the person's help that you were planning to ask for anyway. Becoming very successful you must know the main thing in life is taking action. If you're not taking action into being independent in your day to day life, let alone your goals, you will never acquire that level. Take care of yourself!

8

LEARN A SKILL.

I'm lucky to have a skill. It's called being creative. Creating books, creating content, just creating my own life. But everyone doesn't have the same mindset that I have. I will honestly say I regret not learning a trade. I remember young people used to go to the Job Corps. You learn how to be electricians, plumbers, construction workers and traveled to Hawaii for 6 months to train. That's something I thought about back then. I never took action, but I wish I would have taken up on that offer. It was a low investment that can get you high paying, high quality jobs.

When I mean low Investments I mean time. You can learn to day trade and learn about different things. For example you can become a plumber within less than a year. Once you have these things, from my understanding they do have job placement, but not only that you can go into business for yourself. Learning a skills like this early will pay off exponentially. Let's use buying a house for example. You may be planning to buy a house, or you may even own a house already. Instead of shopping around being ripped off asking or begging people to do tasks to fix things, you will have the skill to actually do the task yourself. You'll be surprised at the amount of information you can learn on YouTube. Try it! Look up anything you want to do. You can learn to play chess, cook, and put things together. Shipping container homes can be found on the internet. I remember when I was young they had something called the "encyclopedia". Now you guys have Wikipedia. Everything is at your fingertips and is easily accessible.

The problem is most people don't take advantage of this. Don't let this be you. You can take full advantage and learn a skill and trade on your own. This can make you money and help you become an entrepreneur even if you work a nine-to-five. If you love something, monetize it! You can also have something to teach your loved ones or your family and it gives you time to bond with them. I remember being young my mother taught me how to garden. One day I will have a real nice garden when I purchase some property later on down the line. But this is something that my mother taught me and in contrast I could teach someone else. One day maybe even my own children.

If I did have children, one thing I wish I could teach them is to live in the NOW. Most importantly however, is to live for the future as well. There needs to be a balance between the two. A lot of times people, even myself have made a lot of decisions when I was younger that I didn't think would affect me today. Remember that decisions that you make today will affect your future. Live in the moment and enjoy what's happening because that will make for your experience in life to be better. However, think before you do and realize what decisions will affect you later. The easiest example I can think of this is teenage pregnancy. Sex is fun, but 18 years with the wrong person can be a decision that can alter your life. I'm not here to be your daddy but I do want to tell you that the amount of resources are out there.

If you didn't take full advantage of this lane you deserve what you get. Stop wasting all your time watching TV. Netflix and chilling and watching things with no substance and discover how to do something. Let's look at it like this. A woman loves a man good with his hands. But a man also loves a woman that's good with her hands also. You get my point, learn to use your brain, use your hands and learn a skill or a trade that can help you become independent, make some money, and you can teach others. Maybe one day you will become Your Own Boss!!!

9.

MONETIZE YOUR HOBBIES

T his is something that you are really learning from my failures. Monetizing your hobbies is one of the most important things you can do in your life. We always hear about getting on our purpose and finding out what we want to do in life. A lot of people do find their purpose rather be teaching, construction, opening up a daycare, anything that they enjoy doing and can monetize. But don't get it confused, some people have a purpose which is making money. You see a lot of people with nine-to-five jobs who make lucrative incomes but are unhappy and stressed.

That's one of the reasons I want to create content full-time. Becoming a principal would be the fastest six-figure income I obtain other than trading, real estate etc just pure career wise. But it can be a stressful day, long hours, basically you are an educator/authority of the teachers and manager of the staff. You have to deal with a lot of different attitudes, problems, and conflicts that you have nothing to do with on a daily basis. This is a job that I felt that I could handle, actually I knew I could handle.

On the flip side however I could put the same amount of time in obtaining that goal and put it into myself. Even though I will have that nice job, the only person not making it riches, is the most important person who's doing all the work, which is me. Monetizing your hobbies is putting yourself in the driver seat, putting your life in your hands and making it become your oyster. Whatever happiness that you have, think about how you can make money from it. If you like reading the paper, become an editor. If you like architecture, figure out how you can maybe build some houses. If you are an artist instead of just drawing when you're bored, sell art and make money from it. I create content on different channels. I have a food channel, a gaming channel and a wrestling channel. Everything that I like to do I already found a way to market myself and make money and or resources at a minimum. You'll be surprised at the amount of people, from all walks of life who like to watch food content.

You may not have all your ideas together but after this reading I want you to exercise writing down your 10 top things. You will figure out which you can monetize, how quick and what the ceiling on this is. When they say when you find something you are really passionate about you don't work a day in your life that is 100% true. I could create content to help others, coach etc for free. The fact that I can get paid for it is a bonus. To be honest with you, the money is a gift for my time. Yes I would like to do it for free, but the monetary aspect keeps me going. It motivates me to create because I know people appreciate what I produce. Whatever, you fight, play sports, find out that you like doing Etc. Find a way to make money with it! Since I mentioned that, let's talk about sports really quick. The chances of becoming a pro athlete I feel people depend on. It's a dream. I want to play basketball, football and baseball etc. I'm not trying to tell you to quit your dreams, but I'm telling you that these are far-fetched because of the ratio of people who actually make it to the Major Leagues.

Lucky for you I have good news for you. You can be involved in sports without playing them yourself. Why do you think retired athletes always go to commentary? Because they get a lucrative salary for something that they like to talk about. Plus as a bonus they get to withhold the same status as they did when they played. Even if it's something simple like being a janitor. Don't be a janitor for 15 to 25 years for someone else, acquire the skills and the discipline and even look at what your manager does. If you acquire enough skills and experience, sooner or later you will be able to run your own business. Not only that ,working in a field year after year you should have also acquired good resources and connections with people that may be even able to work for you! If you want to waste your time doing anything in life, figure out how It can make you some money!!!! If money isn't your form of happiness, I guarantee you it gives you options and comfort. This is not debatable! So let's get it!

10

SAVE. INVEST. BUY PROPERTY

I remember a long time ago I was 19 years old. This was back in the 90s. So anyways I had my own place and three cars. I had an apartment that was passed down to me from my older sister. So this was a 4-Plex, actually there was a small house in the back so what would you call 5. Anyways I thought I was living the life. Why, because my rent was $650. Try that in California, let alone the Eastbay nowadays. You can't even rent a bathroom for that much. On the side where I live it'll cost you a half a million dollars just to get a one bedroom one bath. So now the mindset that I have now is, I wasn't living the life. You see that building could have been mine three four times over again if I had known what I know now. Please don't make the mistakes from my failures. I wish it could go back in time sometimes!

When you're young, start saving your money. Once you have enough money to flip two or three times then you start to invest. There's a key thing: make sure you saved six months to a year worth of salary before you invest. Some people say for one or two months and invest in something and cross their fingers. When you save for investment you want to strategically do so. Buying real estate is one of the most efficient ways to get rich. If you look at all the millionaires in the world there are a lot of moguls that started in real estate. It's the best money you can spend and invest because you're always going to get your money back and more. Just as long as you have patience and can wait out the time. Start putting money in retirement from your first couple of jobs early that way you will have something for a rainy day. I know for the school district you can retire after 20 years regardless if you're 65 or not. Start looking at YouTube content about how deals are made. Watch Real Estate shows! They will give you a lot of valuable information if you take the entertainment aspect out of it. If I could do it all over again I would have my first house by 23 minimum. You don't have to play catch-up like me. You can own your destiny early and be able to have something to share with your family and have residual income. Also when you purchase property you build equity and can pull out of that property to buy more property. That's another book, but you can take that gem and do your own research.

Don't be stupid like I was. I say the worst investment I ever had was gold teeth. Yes gold is worth money but did I need to spend tens of thousands on teeth in my mouth? Did I need a set with earrings to match for every single day of the week? Boy I was young and dumb, but I was chasing what was popular at the time, and it was a ignorant choice. If you know of someone who is financially free or good with money, become their best friend. If you hang around them enough you probably won't even have to ask for their help they'll be willing to teach you. A lot of people that are good in business look for someone that they can pass the information down to. Just like myself, I'm willing to teach anyone but they have to be willing to learn and to listen. Be good at learning and listening and you acquire knowledge to influence your desires. Save your money, learn game, search for resources to obtain real estate & property. Remember you don't have to wait till you're old to do this, start young. Be better than me.

11.

DONT LOOK FOR LOVE VALIDATION

C oaching for years I noticed a few patterns. I always teach you guys to acknowledge patterns and search for the configuration. This is one that I pattern I consistently found. People need validation. Women need validation from men. Men need validation from women. Women need validation from other women. And men need the validation of other men. This is real life and this is what goes on. It is the making of human nature. However when you look for the validation of others you always sell yourself short. It's okay for people to validate you if you're good at something, good looking, or performed a nice gesture. The key is not to look for it. If you are validated within yourself everything that someone tells you outside that is a bonus.

The more you look for validation from other people, the more you'll be disappointed. I'm going to say something very hard but very true. People will turn on you and at the end of the day you might as well make yourself happy because in an instant people will unfollow you like instagram but in real life. Don't stress yourself out trying to make yourself look good for other people who really don't care about you at the end of the day. If they do care about you it's just about their need of you or maybe what you're bringing to the table. The more you validate yourself the more happy you will be. The more happy that you are the more you can help people because of your good spirit and your aspiring to others. Celebrate YOU!

Relationships are a crucial validation. A lot of women for example, want to feel validation for being in a relationship sacrificing their happiness. What do I mean by this? Well there's lots of people who are happy on Facebook and Instagram but are miserable in real life. They literally live their life for validation for other people. I remember I was traveling one day and people were more in tune with taking pictures in front of the monument then actually enjoying the moment. It's like they weren't even there. The only moment they were experiencing was them taking the picture and the validation that they would get after they post it. Again, you go out of your way to impress your Facebook friends then what happens when Facebook shuts down. No more validation. You must be the one to validate yourself, but remember there must be something to validate.

This will be such an easy task if you work on your purpose and things that you enjoy. If you have projects and goals and see progression it will give you a happy spirit and positive energy. It will make you feel good and it also will encourage and inspire you to accomplish more goals to continue this feeling. You are one person and you know how you feel inside. Never let any relationship between husband wife, even your mother and father tell you how you should feel about yourself. I'm the type of person who really only values people's opinions that I respect. That's because people that respect you will tell you things to help you rather than scrutinize or pop your balloon of joy.

Look out for jealous people too. Jealous people will always try to pick apart everything you do and give you suggestions without acknowledging the good you did. Ever noticed that? Yeah I know, they're quick to tell you what you can change to make better without acknowledging what you did right. Stay away from those types of people. Also there's truth in jokes and people who always talk about you in a malicious way, or always want to joke and say they're just playing, they're serious. Stay away from those types of people as well. It will take from your energy and success. Internal validation is the best feeling, when you wake up and tell yourself you're the SHIT in the mirror and really feel it! Get your head out of the sand and start accomplishing goals and pursue your dreams. Remember that being successful doesn't matter how much money you bring in, houses, cars etc, because all that can be taken away from you in an instant. It has to start with you first so make sure you do your work within. Keep your head up and always continue to move forward. Never look for validation from others, be an expert at validating yourself.

12.

MASTERSOLITUDE

Mastering Solitude is something that I did naturally. People always call me an introvert but are confused about how outgoing I am. I love to interact with other people, however I love my space as well. This put me in the space where I was never needy. I can literally be at home all week not be bothered by the phone and be pleasant just reading and learning from YouTube. Mastering solitude doesn't mean staying in the house either. You need to be content with your own presence. Your own thoughts, goal-setting, planning or things you can do when you're in solitude.

The best way to make plans is to have no distraction in solitude. I remember I mastered solitude when I started a monk mode. If you don't know what that is that's basically when you unplug and you start learning about yourself. People think "monk mode" is just not dating and having sex with women. Nope, monk mode is finding out what you want to do in life, finding that plan and moving towards that. How this worked for me was I got so invested in my goals and the process of becoming successful that everything hit the back side. It totally killed my dating life because going on dates wasn't conducive to me making money and building towards my future. Writing on my books, educating myself, was more important on going during dinner dates and hanging out. So, it can have its ups and downs but in life there needs to be balance in everything that you do. If you master solitude you never have to worry about being a "yes man" or a pushover. People that are comfortable entertaining themselves and enjoy their own company are strong people at heart. They can take or leave people. This is a strong stance to have in any relationship and if you want an abundance mindset this is the first strategy to conquer in order to obtain that.

The last thing I want to say about mastering solitude is this. Don't wait for a drastic situation! For instance your mother dying, you losing your job, or break up/ divorce. The reason being is you can go into a situation trying to master solitude, but leave solitude dark and face depression. Make sure when you attempt to master solitude have a goal in mind or something particular that you want to get out of it. I would suggest even writing that thing down. Don't be in the situation where you're depressed wanting to see or avoid everyone in life and call that mastering solitude. You are going to soak in your own emotions, become depressed and never win or be able to conquer everything in life. You won't accomplish anything, and you won't be able to attract anything positive because of your negative behavior, body language, and mindset. You think people can't see it because it's your mind. Energy is powerful! Don't be surprised when people can feel your energy. It can repulse them like roaches on the kitchen floor in the middle of the night. In relationships, it's always good to have another half, but mastering solitude will have you wanting that person, but not needing them. No matter how deep your love is, knowone wants the pressure of feeling like their happiness is coming from validation from another person. Mastering solitude is one of the easiest and simple ways to become whole. Lastly, don't count the days, just enjoy the process. Maybe start in 30-day increments Check in every month to see how you feel. If you have a hard time with structure and foundation, check in every week. I just don't want you counting every minute on the day waiting to get out of it. That would defeat the whole purpose Mastering solitude is the process of self-mastery.

13.

TRAVEL EARLY AND GET YOUR PASSPORT

When it comes to my personality, traveling early would almost be number one on my list . Traveling is a passion of mine. It's something that I do to release. To refresh. In a community we often hear men travel for women sex etc. For me that couldn't be farthest from the truth. I love to be around people of different nationalities just seeing different things. I remember I was in Jamaica cruising the streets of the ghetto, just seeing how these people lived was mind-blowing. Yes I'm here for a few days on vacation but for them this is their everyday way of life. It made me appreciate what I have at home more. The things that I complain about are very minimal.

I started traveling early around the age of 21. I went on a trip by myself to Los Angeles with a woman I met from Myspace. I shared that story in "Finesse Game". You can check that out. Before that though I would go to little car functions. "Hot August Nights" in Reno Nevada, things of that nature. This was basically a car show and a reason for young teenagers to get together and be obnoxious. For women, dress more provocative and seductive than they usually would. It was a hookup culture mainly. As they say cars and women go together. I remember trying to rally up people to travel and go to different places and it would never fall through. It got to a point when that situation in L.A, I just jumped off the bridge and went for it. From then on I started to travel. Then year after year I learn more about myself. It made me make things happen! Being in stranger environments makes you produce. It made my thinking very diverse being around people with different ideologies and they can tell me actually why they think the way they do instead of me making the assumption. That's a side note, traveling alone can even be even more inspiring.

I would suggest one person though that's good enough. Thing is it doesn't even have to be your friend. I've actually met friends through traveling. Shout out to my boy Chris. I met him in Belize, we both traveled solo and we met up later in Dubai. We still talk to this day. Traveling connects you with people with similar mindsets a similar interest as you. Your best friend, husband, or wife may just be a hop, skip, jump, plane or train ride away. Don't wait until someone in your family gets married or for someone that graduates from college to start traveling. The earlier the better.Every time you get paid put money away for flight money. Book yourself a flight, lock yourself in, that way you know that you will go. For people who don't have a passport and you're scared to travel abroad that's fine. Travel from state-to-state. You will be amazed how differently people live. Even when I go camping yearly. For some of those people out there when we white water raft, that's actually their way of life!! They hang out in their own community outside. Hanging out there on the river is just a daily thing not as a vacation as it is to me.

Some of the coolest experiences traveling are walking up the stairs to the Great Wall of China. Going up to the top up of the Empire State Building. Going to the Stadium Colosseum in Rome which was cool in itself but it's also where Bruce Lee film's Infamous fight scenes with Chuck Norris in Return of the Dragon. I've been to Pablo Escobar's Infamous house and his Club. I've been on top of a mountain going down a roller coaster in Haiti. I partied with strippers in Mexico and woke up and didn't remember a thing. I've been chased down by bodyguards behind fooling with Puerto Rican stripperss in Puerto Rico. I've hung out with good friends in Hawaii and toured the streets where Obama was raised. I have been on a helicopter cruised across top the city Las Vegas. I Went Extreme Safari Driving in Dubai. Now this is not to brag, this is to ask yourself a question. This is just a handful of experiences,but do you not think this experience has broadened my horizons and opened my mind to new things? If the answer is no you're wrong of course it did. All these experiences were created in my mind first. I put forth action! These trips are now experiences that I can live through through pictures and videos. I've been documented for the next lifetime! One cool thing I remember is going on a speed boat in a river in Thailand. It took me to a river shop where they made my pho noodles on the boat. Just cool stuff like that beats going to 420 and spending money on tennis shoes, Gucci belts and Louis Vuitton bags the only other woman care about. Travel guys, ladies too. Travel early. Assist others that are willing to help or go with you but don't depend on them, jump out there and do it yourself. Maybe I'll be willing to join you on the next round.

14.

LEARN TO FIGHT

'm sorry to bust your bubble. I don't just watch wrestling UFC and boxing because I like to watch people get their ass kicked. I study on how to kick people's asses. When I was younger me and my friend started a boxing league. There were about 12 of us. We would keep stats records and everything. We were really into it. So basically I could kick everybody's ass. I remember there was an older guy named Jimmy. He was two years older than us. He was rich, he had his house built and he had a grand piano inside of it. He came equipped with all the boxing shit that we had, on top of cooler stuff like taekwondo gear. Being a follower, these guys were hopping right on his jock! He had all the cool stuff. On top of that he had every single game system as well. So we had the boxing League and since he was older he influenced us to make it open it up to

Kickboxing. Which by the way he would murder us all. This ruined my confidence and I started getting in the other things.

The point of that story is just knowing how to fight gives you confidence that can't get bought. No matter how much money you make, how good you are with girls or how good you are at bitcoiners, or you're a cyborg in trading. If you know if someone gets into it with you or you're in trouble you know how to defend yourself and kick someone's ass gives you an ass kicker mentality. It's not that you want trouble but you're not afraid of it. That energy is very attractive to women and men alike. It's also a leader quality when people know that they can count on you to defend them and they'll be willing to fight for you as well. Think of all the good leaders, they're all decent fighters and that's the reason why people will be willing to lead by them. We can formulate and control a gang of Kings or Queens. You have to be in the position of power and have the confidence knowing that you can take somebody out.

In case you guys don't know I was obsessed with wrestling. I would watch all the moves and I would even try to be in shape. I was really good at doing push-ups. I was the push-up King. I was also obsessed with karate. Bruce Lee was my favorite! I practiced all his moves, hand gestures and sound effects. I persuaded my mother to put me in kung fu. I got pretty good at it. I had a little issue. The problem was, I didn't get into it because it wasn't what I saw on TV. It was more of the defense. I wanted to kick people's asses. I thought all karate was the same later on so I figured out the different styles and techniques. I've also been very interested in Muay Thai and want to take that up soon maybe professionally later on down the line. That's just a side note, something that I was always interested in wanted to do. Even in video games I always took a liking to the Thai fighters. Fighting with their knees and elbows attacking very aggressively. If I'm going through life and I'll have a knowone will mess with me. I can give him a spinning back fist that will give me an ass-kicker my vibe and energy, people will second-guess trying to shuffle with me.

Ladies and gentlemen it is very imperative that you learn to defend yourself. You cannot go through life having a scarcity mindset or scarcity as far as being a victim to conflict. Learning to stand up for yourself will give you confidence and energy that will attract similar mindsets! Your energy will also detract weak people that only entertain people that are less than them. Also learning to fight can also keep you in good shape as well if you take it seriously. There's a couple of older MMA fighters that I liked, following a pattern myself like them. Not necessarily to be world champion but just to use mixed martial arts as a way to keep my body looking right and my body tight. Life is full of conflict, be prepared in case something happens and learn to fight!

15.

HAVE FRIENDS ALL ETHNICITIES

Speaking of childhood, a major key is to have friends of all races. Being able to relate to diverse situations is key to our success. There are circumstances that are made to be exceptions but for the most part when you're successful you deal with every kind of person. Every kind of mindset, with different kinds of background. So why not try to connect to as many people as possible, that way you can relate to them. For those of you that don't know I grew up in the suburbs. Very diverse! One of a few honey blacks in my school. My hobbies consisted of art drawing, dressing nicely, riding my bike and building tree houses. When I was young, I was a master of video games as well. My friends range from all races. I had Hawaiin friends, rainbow friends, White, Asian, and Mexican friends. This is throughout my life.

Even up to now it helps me teach kids because I've been around every race. I understand different struggles and how different families are set up. When I came to Oakland Ca, in Middle School it was a culture shock and I had to quickly learn and adjust to my environment being predominantly black. The interests that I had in the white environment were not cool to the black kids. So I had to adapt to what they did. When I was young my hobbies were baseball and soccer. I did have the boxing league but that was in the neighborhood. As far as school goes, baseball and soccer is the thing that we did. So in Oakland it was more about football and basketball. That's why I never was good at basketball because at the time everyone else had been playing since they were young and we didn't play basketball where I grew up. Matter of fact I only watched basketball from my mother. Her ex-husband played professionally overseas which made her a fan.

We didn't even have basketball courts at school, funny I never thought about that until now.

That's why they say college is the best place to network. Because you're put in a place where a lot of people come from different places all with similar goals. The degree, or whatever field that you are pursuing. Never be afraid to put yourself out there and meet new people. Some of my best friends I've ever had in life we're not black. On top of that some of the best friends that I like and laugh at in life we didn't have similar interests, but similar quirky personalities. It's okay whatever race you are to have self pride and integrity for your ethnicity I get it. Just be open to new people because they'll teach you new things. Besides seafood some of my favorite foods are tacos. As we know tacos are not black food. Had I not been exposed to that I wouldn't be enjoying the favorite thing I like to eat. Funny thing is that African American food is what I eat the least. I would say Asian food a lot. I have a taste bud for salt and pepper often. The point is to meet different people from different backgrounds and ethnicities and be open to their experiences as you can learn about yourself. The person that you may need to help you advance in life may not be the same color as you. If the person who you may want to be your other half wife or husband or be the partner to raise your kids with may not be the same color as you either. Be open to this and experience all a life as let it as it is here open for you.

16.

FOCUS ON POSITIVE ENERGY AND MINDSET

ocus on your positive energy. After studying human behavior for the last 20 or so years I picked up on energy and how important it is. I've always been aware but now I have it down to a science. I remember one of my favorite movies, Two Can Play That Game. The main character Morris Chestnut was in a relationship with Vivica Fox when she broke up with him. He tried to get her over the phone and he was stressed out because she would neglect him. Finally he got through and went with the date. He pulled up to her house and they engaged in physical contact very quickly. He was able to transfer the energy. Now she was upset and he left feeling more pleasant. This is a perfect visual of what energy is and how it could be transferred. From one person to another. Negative people usually surround themselves with other negative people. The same way as positive people surround yourself with people that are positive or at least have winter mindsets.

I can guarantee you that having positive energy will guarantee you people that you need around in life. Have you ever met anyone to be like damn they are always happy. They're always smiling. Or some people you just like talking to whether it be a family member, or that person at work, that always makes you laugh. Crazy right. It's crazy because this person can be you. You can control your energy! Just as you can control your mind and the things that you do. Instead of crying playing victim, use the negative experiences in your life to make yourself better. A lot of people have similar circumstances but only certain ones get out of it correctly and make the necessary changes. Example, a lot of us come from single-family parent homes including myself. Some people use it as a crunch for failure or some people use that to fuel their success. I don't cry about not having a father. I use that as fuel to provide for my mother. I want to be successful so I can provide my mother a better lifestyle. You see, that's all energy and a mindset.

Bruce Lee talks a lot about energy in his movies. Actually I think he might have imprinted me with it as his movies were made in the 70s and I will see them in my early eighties and childhood. They say that the ages of three or four is where you can really obtain in withhold information. The same way kids that are young age learn multiple languages. It's something that I always knew, but I couldn't really point or remember where I got it from. When you go to rallies or strikes people are usually talking crazy or emotional in their energy because they're hurt. It's the same way when you are at a funeral. You may not be crying, but the energy in the room of everybody in their emotions make you feel their emotions as well. Energy is so strong you can feel it through TV. Think about watching a movie and seeing the sad part.... It will make you cry. When your favorite character dies, it will make you shed tears of someone that you've never even met. Energy controls emotion. Always remember that. The great thing is, if you can control your energy you can control your emotions. If you can control your emotions you control your mindset. And if you control all these things then you control you, and you become a master of yourself. Focus on receiving and getting positive energy. Energy that is on a lower frequency of yours dispose of it. When you deal with people in life always ask yourself is this person that asset or a liability. If you consider someone to be a liability in your life unless they are your sick grandparents, or friends re-evaluate that relationship. In life you need only assets to grow to be the best. When you watch TV or watch people throughout life study the habits of very positive people. You will notice that they speak on energy as well because it's a universal thing. Your energy has no shape, size, or expectation, other than you controlling how high or low it can be.

17.

PREY. MEDITATE.UNPLUG

Every week I take a day to do nothing. I suggest you do the same. When I say unplug I mean no TV and phone. I would only suggest reading is the thing that you can do when you're unplugging because you are opening your mind to knowledge. I will suggest everyone meditate or at least try it. If not every single day, maybe once a week to reflect on the week and plan for the next week. Meditating helps you control your energy, your thoughts, and your vibe in general. We all get caught up in life and day-to-day interactions. Life, family, job stress, financial, emotions Etc. Take one day to unplug. If you can afford more, then I will suggest that as well.

But don't use unplug as a way to be lazy. It's just nice to gather your thoughts and plan in a pleasant place in your mind from time to time. Life can get busy. We all understand this just takes a time to take the time out.

Just think of it like sports; they have to take breaks in order to figure out what their next move is.

So in life make sure you take your timeouts. Use them wisely though. You make the best decisions in life with lots of rest and a clear open mind. That this is how depression comes about. People become overwhelmed first. Then later on they become stressed. When they're stressed out they become even more overwhelmed and make quick, fast, and bad decisions. This will result in unsuccessful actions and will put people in the dark depressing state. They will be depressed and hide in darkness from their failures. Trust and believe there's plenty of resources on YouTube or online. If you are a person who has no religion maybe you didn't grow up in the church, try anything abnormal to sample different cultures. You don't have to be born into religion you can pick and choose what reflects you and your ideologies. Think Malcolm X. or Mike Tyson. Try out different churches as well.

Just have a time to reflect on everything that you do. Also take time to figure out what your purpose is and also we evaluate your purpose. I stated previously you don't have to be in any type of religion either but just try different things. Be open and if you don't like things just simply don't do them again... Easy. No matter how busy your life is, take time and unplug. Rent a hotel room just to think, plan and strategize. Relax and take the bubble bath you may not be able to make at home. I guarantee you every time you unplug when you go back, to reassure your task, you will feel refreshed. That's what the weekend is supposed to be used for, but our day-to-day life sometimes lets that not happen. Make time for a time out. Unplug for a moment...

18

GET A PET

I would suggest everyone have a pet in their life. I swear I have had my dog Lincoln for 3 years now and he's one of the best blessings that ever happened to me. He showed me what unconditional love is and how it is to nurture and care for something and that loves you back unconditionally. Now this is my first dog, but I remember growing up I did have pet fish. Just me feeding them, gave me responsibility every day. Naming them, figuring out their personalities gave me a sense of being a parent without having the joy of making the baby. At the time I didn't get it, but now that I'm older I realize the importance of having your pet. It could be a cat, dog, raccoon, monkey, whatever you're into that's on you. I just know that having a pet teaches you unconditional love and responsibility. The best part about this is you don't have to be a grown up to have it. If I were to have kids at this point in my life I would make sure that my kids have pets. We would probably start with something small like a fish or a turtle etc. As my kid gets older, then maybe I'll build on something with more personality, and up the responsibility.

Also it will give them an imagination because they can interact with something that can't talk back to them. Things like this when you were young shows you how to think and use your imagination for someone. Especially a pets personality. It wouldn't be able to express it to you. It's just cool things like this that you can expose yourself to at any age, so why not indulge. This is for men and women included. I will suggest you getting a pet at any age, whatever you're into. Even if it's a tiny bird, get something. Are you single? It will keep you company and you won't be worried about getting ghosted or sending out texts. Wasting energy paying attention to people who don't care about you, and don't want your company, because you have your own with your pet. I am a pet owner and I will suggest everyone invest in getting a pet. If you are a parent, invest in getting a pet of your child or your choice for your children as well. It can teach them lifelong lessons and give them a heart, responsibility, and feel true love. Even to this day, when I travel it's harder now because I have to accommodate my dog as if he was my child. Knowing you have something to take care of makes you more responsible and you make less selfish sporadic decisions.

19.

DOCUMENT THE JOURNEY

Documenting your life is something cool. Seeing that I'm an author/ content creator where this comes automatic. People often comment on some of my older videos. When I look at the video to comment back I can look at the video images and it puts me at that particular place in time. The way I look, my hairstyles even the way that I dress is funny and I can make a mockery of it. With social media we basically are in the age where we are documenting our lives. You can scroll on your old threads and see pictures from 2013 and see how different style is to what you wear today. As common as social media seems, everyone isn't on social media. I think everyone should take advantage of this. It's networking, which is as far as documenting your thoughts, accomplishments, desires etc. A lot of famous people will do something spectacular and they'll have their old tweets to back up their statements years ago.

Things that I say right now I committed to earlier and have the footage! Before my YouTube channel and after. Take as many pictures as you can look at life as you want to leave as much stuff for your grandkids etc. Don't you like looking at old photo albums to experience the novelty of seeing your parents when they were young married and love etc? Your grandparents, when they met at the miniature golf course. Whatever it is, document what you can. They didn't have as many options back then as they do now, abuse your power!. It's a good way to bookmark your success as well. If you're trying to get in shape, documenting your success with pictures is the best way to motivate yourself. If you know you didn't lose weight that you were supposed to, you'll be motivated the next week to do better. You should document your life pictures, writing journals, everything. Do a lot of cool stuff so that when you're long gone people can get a sense of Who You Are by your words, establishments, achievements and hopefully pictures or video content. Document your path to success and one of those days that you take a timeout when you unplug, enjoy what you used to be and look forward to what you will become.

20

CAMP AND EXPLORE THE OUTDOORS

C amping and going outdoors is something that seems regular but a lot of people aren't exposed to. People dont go outside and play anymore! I grew up in the suburbs as a child and as a teenager moving forward to adulthood I was in the city. I wasn't exposed to nature really that much. I do remember my mother taking me to the parks of course like any other kid and we would go camping but I was so young. I remember when I got reintroduced to the outdoors I was just taking walks. When I moved to the bay area I would frequent the marina. Where I grew up, in the suburbs we didn't have that. I remember as a teenager they would have these functions at Lake Berryessa and Lake Camanche. When the party guys would drink and smoke on boats that was basically a hookup for whatever your vice. But it was outdoors, and we would have fun BBQs playing music etc.

It's something that's free, doesn't cost you anything, but you can get everything from. On a side note from learning and exposing yourself to outdoors you should also learn to swim too. When I was young swimming was second nature. Everyone had a pool. The weather would become very hot so it was absolutely needed!

Even me being a bigger guy people would be surprised by how well of a swimmer I was because of my size. Not knowing that was one of my childhood activities. Swimming can help you stay in shape and one day, even Save a Life! Learn to swim. As far as outdoors by the water, lake , river, camping it just makes you respect nature. Respect things that grow around you in life that have nothing to do with you. Animals have their own existence, friends, mates, and everything in their environment, that's pretty cool. It's one thing going to the museum or the zoo but you're only seeing animals in fake elements of their environment or in cages. It's just like seeing your favorite player play a home game. Seeing them in their natural environment you will respect and enjoy animals more. It will also give you survivor skills, knowing how to cook ,starting a fire, swimming as I earlier mentioned etc, are skills needed in case something drastic were to happen. Every year I go whitewater rafting with friends. It's exhilarating, exciting and it's something that I look forward to every year. Again if I were to have kids this would absolutely be something I would expose them to.

I'll even use river rafting as an example. When you go outdoors you have the opportunity of the raft most likely. I like to Whitewater raft personally. You usually ride a Whitewater raft with a team of people. What happens if it teaches you Teamwork because you have to depend on each other to get down the White Water stream. Everyone has to be focused and in sync. In contrast you also have to be a very good listener to hear your instructor through the rapid waters. Team building experiences can help your life as well as being a good listener and a learner. This will help you become a good teacher later on. Don't be obsessed with shows like Survivor have the experience yourself.

The water, the air, everything it just smells different out there. Don't just take my word for it, get out there and hit the outdoors and see what it has to offer. Make sure you do some animal watching as well..

21

SKY DIVE

eaven is by far the best experience I had in my life. Imagine you're up all night looking at YouTube videos. Trying to garner the experience of jumping out of a plane 18,000 feet in the air. It doesn't matter how much you look at stuff you cannot feel what an experience is. That's because it's not an experience. I know it may sound crazy. I understand people who have children, you're saying "hell no I'm not jumping out of the plane". Trust me, you have just the same amount of chance getting in an airplane accident as you do falling from skydiving. For one you can't even jump out of a plane anyway by yourself. People tend to think that they just take you up in the air, strap you with a pair of shoes and let you do it your way. Know you're with a highly trained professional who's trained many hours to to handle people just like you on a daily basis. This is a situation where as deep as I want to get into telling you how it is, you have to actually do it yourself. Shout out to my brother RPC we just had a discussion about this. What I told him was the best way you can imagine skydiving is two things. The first thing is you don't fall, you float. Imagine yourself driving on the highway. Let's push the gas down at 80 miles per hour. You stick your hand out of there. The way the wind shuffles your hand back and forth is the way that you feel when you're falling. So take that feeling and reverse it to a down horizontal feeling. That's all it pretty much is. I will say once you get up there and you see the person before you jump it's a little scary. If you're that scared just close your eyes. Once you jump off that plane you feel love, and every emotion when you're looking at your life before you. It's like Superman, when he comes from another planet and sees Earth. That's how you see the world. It makes you reflect on everything that's non-existent and makes you realize what's important. Once they pull that string expect a little snug and they levitate you. Then you coast left and right swaying in the sky watching everything and your accomplishments including the one you just did! When you hit the floor you'll think damn I did it. I did something that wasn't meant to do. It's almost like you broke a law or a record. You seem like you're living life on overtime now and you were giving extra time to do something creative. I would also suggest having this experience with someone else that way when you talk about it, you and that person can have your own bubble and relate to each other. Again it's an experience that can't really be explained, you just have to do it yourself. I did my best to try and give you the vision! Jumping out of a plane will change your life for the better. It's not like jumping off a building. Get that narrative out of your head. If you can jump down a flight of stairs trust me you can jump out of a plane. Now this is about the best $250 I've ever spent. We always speak about abundance mindset. If you want a quick cheat sheet on how to get it, jump out of a plane and come talk to me after. You can't convince me you won't feel like top shit and you can conquer anything.

If you can jump out of a plane, you mean to tell me you can't pass a test? If you can jump out of a plane, you mean to tell me you can't get over a breakup? If you jump out of a plane you mean to tell me you can't get a new job after you've been fired? Sounds oxymoron right? That's because it is. If you want an abundance mindset and you want to live life to the fullest knowing you can conquer anything. Invest in yourself, go tandem skydiving and it will change your life. If you ask 10 people who actually went skydiving themselves, not their cousin, not what the Granddad told them, but themselves lol. I can almost assure you that they'll tell you the same exact thing that I said. Jumping out of a plane is like being in a private club. It's kind of like the Illuminati. A club of winners, risk takers, and people with an abundance mindset who are willing to put it all on the line. That's what being a skydiver tells other people who shared a similar experience as you have. If you want to pop your cherry look for the local "iFly" and try that out. I will tell you that it's nothing compared to the real thing.

Make your first jump! The quicker the better! No, I didn't get paid for this advertisement ... If this book does however sell millions of copies, iFly cut the check guys!

22

PLAY GRAND THEFT AUTO

This is one of the last keys. Grand Theft Auto is an open-ended playground. Remember life is just a reflection of the choices that you make. Make choices that reflect what you think, and what you're willing to discover. Think of yourself as the main character of Grand Theft Auto. Yes you have missions, and I'm not promoting anyone to kill people. Actually I think Grand Theft Auto is negative for kids to be able to manipulate murder, drugs, prostitution and every other crime known to man, but that's another book in another chapter. What I will say is that in Grand Theft Auto there's open-ended missions. What does this mean for you?

It means you can create your own circumstances. You can create your own destiny. Just like Grand Theft Auto. If you want to work on your attributes, for example in the game you can lift weights, and put in the work to build a better body, or attract more women. If you want money to save for something, you do side jobs and save your money.

You can walk up to strangers and have conversation and meet friends. You network with different people to accomplish different goals. All this is not a video game. This is your life! Your life is literally a video game and you can control it. The difference between life and video is video games are controlled by you, not emotion. So if you're able to control your emotions and your energy, just think of the video game for yourself and your life that you can create. Every good creator, successful and famous people had a dream just like you do. They had a thought and your desire. The way you feel right now reading this book. The difference between them is they signed up to live for that moment, and let that desire push them to the next level.

Get it, Next Level!!. Whatever level you want in life, know that if you truly work on your attributes, study and learn new skills you can get to the new level of your desires. Just like playing the video game, it takes hard work, dedication most importantly a lot of time and consistency. Play Grand Theft Auto in real life! It takes hours, upon hours, upon hours of time. You have to work! Prepare to play Grand Theft Auto with your life. Just keep the violence part for the video game!

23

WRITE A BOOK

Now that I'm an author of multiple books, people hit me up about how to write and structure their thoughts. Well guess what? I finessed the hell out of you. Why would you say that question? Because each one of these chapters gives routes and you reflect about how you felt about each principal as well as your action plan. So now you have an active sheet of how to navigate your life, things that you should know, and be willing to learn. Take all these pieces together and now you formulated the chapter of your own book. Throughout this, keep learning, read, listen, comprehend and most importantly write your goals down. Most people aren't successful because they write their goals down with no plan. They only hope to get what they desire. They have no action plan of how to get there. Now YOU hold your desires, feelings and reflections for the rest of your life, as well as an action plan to get there. Life has no guarantees.

However I will guarantee, if you follow this plan to a T, you will improve exponentially at a minimum. It's like any book that you've read,or any movie that you have watched. Understand that there will be Ups and Downs. Trials and Tribulations. There will be times where you want to fall and give up. Times where you feel like you're down, and knowone (at least it feels like) can understand the way that you feel. The key is to sign up for the end result of your life. Then figure out the best plan in your map to get there. Learn to tell your own story!

24.

ENJOY BUT DON'T GET ATTACHED

E njoy, don't get attached! This can literally save your life. Most of the hardships that you have in life, losing a job, family loss, a divorce, all equals attachment. People don't know how to enjoy things without being attached to them. Yes this can be very difficult but if you plan anything, you can see everything. Remember you look at other people's stories. People who have got married two or three times, did a lot of cool stuff, but never got attached to one thing. Is very imperative to follow this principle; it can ruin your life if you don't. I've seen this analogy used plenty of times but just let me be the new person to use it. If you went to the doctor and we're told that you have one year of life what would you do?

If you live your life like this you will start doing things you never thought she would do. Appreciate experiences like you never have prior. Even spending time with people you thought she wouldn't. You will face your fears and start living life more abundant. My father died of cancer when I was three. I felt like when he knew he was dying he probably was active as possible, because he knew death was coming soon. No one wants to live in regret, and if there's things in life that you don't accomplish at least be able to let yourself know that you tried. When, or if you have kids they may ask you about a particular thing. Wouldn't you rather say son or daughter I tried to but (insert the story)... Rather than saying I feared that and I shied away because I was afraid. You can't teach someone to be strong when you fear something yourself. Especially when other people can target what your weaknesses and fears are. Don't be a coward. Stand up and face your fears!

No relationship lasts forever. Even people who are married. To you spectators who will say "two people have died at the same time"that's not actually true. Maybe by seconds. The point is when one person leaves the earth you're alone. So enjoy the person, the things that are tangible or intangible experience while It was here. Be able to let go. If it's your favorite car and someone tows it, don't go jump off a bridge! Be able to let go and remember the memories. If your dog runs away, remember the memories and the good times. Maybe you'll learn to be more attentive to the next pet that you get. Your dog won't be able to run away. You learned from your failure. Learn from your mistakes, that's the lesson in this book. You're learning principles that I know later on in my life. I wish that I knew these before learning now. I am convinced, it is all in this book for you to have, all in one place. Life lessons are the things that helped my mindset and energy grow strong and wise beyond my years to motivate others. I will take the responsibility to live a positive life! That way I can influence people from years on all across the globe.

Remember, I jumped out of that plane? So I'm living on spare time. Don't mope around in your negative experiences, trauma family. We know that you lack money, resources, common sense and education (sarcasm). Remember this is Grand Theft Auto, you're in control of that! Start taking side missions and look at that map! When you push the pausebutton, you will be able to see your whole journey as well as the destination in order to figure out your best path to get there. Remember everything that you do, ups and downs, reflect, make adjustments and enjoy it. Not only the wins and the luxury, also embrace the pain as well. If you can still breathe, you can still get up and try again. Also, you can tell and teach others what not to do! Teach them what lessons you learned, as I'm teaching you the lessons for my failures.

25.

LOVE YOURSELF

This is the main key. Quick, easy, short and to the point. People look for love to make them feel better. You will never attract love if you don't love yourself. If you are able to do this, it will only be temporary. And if it's longer than temporary, you will end up in a codependent relationship. Knowone wants to feel responsible for someone else's happiness. Don't put yourself in that position because that is not giving real love. When you love yourself to completeness you can truly love others. You can love, with no judgement, entitlement and show appreciation for strangers and even your enemies! Some people may feel so damaged that they cannot love themselves. Just like anything it's all about commitment. I can't change your past, but you my friend, can change your future. We comprehend that this will be a long miraculous journey! As of today, commit to the job of loving yourself. Then others and life as a whole, will love you better!

EPILOGUE

I created this book to summarize things that I've learned from mistakes that I've made. It's kind of like a cheat sheet. Also I wanted to make it very digestible for people of any age or background. I have multiple books of different genres. "The Keys" for example is a personal development book. Personal development is my niche but for its most definitely not for everyone. It doesn't have to be and you should be ok with that! The "Dominance Mindset" is a book for dating; everyone isn't in the dating books. This however is something that it complies to everyone. No matter what race, size, color,if you are practicing the principles in this book, applying the energy to your mindset and the strategies we've discussed.

It will touch you! Open your soul up the same way you open your heart for love! You will help you become a better person. It doesn't matter how busy your schedule is, you can read a chapter or two a day and be able to actively pursue your goals and dreams with this action plan that I created for you. Actually we did it together! You now have it created for yourself and you are now the author of your environment! We went through all the steps, figured out your dreams and what your passion is by positive reflection. I want to give you pat on the back, because you always had the key the entire time. I just helped you make sure the key fit! So that you can open the chest to receive your crown that you now will receive! Thank you for taking the time out to read this, and I hope I will help you cut corners and eliminate future mistakes. Focus on becoming great! Share this book with someone you love and have them pass it around, and pay it forward as well. More successful mindsets, create more positive people and energy! We all are in charge of producing the best out of the world. The problem is we spend too much time watching everybody else. There are three types of people. Watchers, Talkers and People who Get Shit Done!!! Finishers! Remember it all starts off with you.

SUDDEN DEATH FREE GAME

Thi is some "sudden death free game" that can help you out in life instantly. Something that you can apply to your day-to-day life. This is actually something new in my repertoire that I just started and I'd like to share this secret with you. This is a gesture that's very simple but highly effective. Give yourself a number greater than 10. Challenge yourself to do 10 or more things today. You can choose a number like 21, that's all up to you as long as it's at least 10. These things could consist of doing the laundry, washing the dishes, or paying off bills that you've been neglecting.

It can be something like taking yourself on a hike. Use this to try something new. Try reading a book that you normally wouldn't read. Or creating conversation with people that you normally wouldn't talk to. If you challenge yourself to 10 new things per day you will like the feeling of accomplishing these many goals. As you continue to conquer 10 things add a few more .This will stop you from putting things to the side. One of the reasons why we aren't successful is because we put things off to the next day. The next day becomes the next week. Then rinse and repeat. Make 10 daily challenges and mark them off. Watch and see how your confidence grows and how more productive your days will be. You will live to chase new and spectacular goals, because you are a winner, and you have an abundance mindset! Being productive is a major key to becoming successful in anything that you do. So after you read this, don't start monday morning, don't start in the morning, Start right now!!!!!

THANK YOU....

Peace and blessings to you all Kings and Queens. I have shown you the Key to your Crown. Wear it proudly. You earned it! You are now royalty! Time to start a Kingdom of your own...

MY INSPIRATION

T he following pages are letters to me from my father. He knew he was dying from cancer. So what he did was whip out that calligraphy pen and teach me from his failures and lessons. From the age of three up until the age of twenty one he wrote me a long heartfelt letter letting me know where I should be and what I should be focused on. I'm sure he did a lot of reflecting on his life as well! Every year my mother would distribute my letter like a birthday card. She would read them to me and as time went on I would read them to her. This is my same vision for you as the reader. I'm paying it forward! I practice what I preach! The wisdom and lessons my father taught me, even after he passed away will touch many! He touched me and showed me how to help others as well as structure and develop myself. I will openly share some with you. Enjoy!

Made in the USA
Monee, IL
10 June 2021

70884668R00066